Shoe Box Learning Centers

Science

by Immacula A. Rhodes

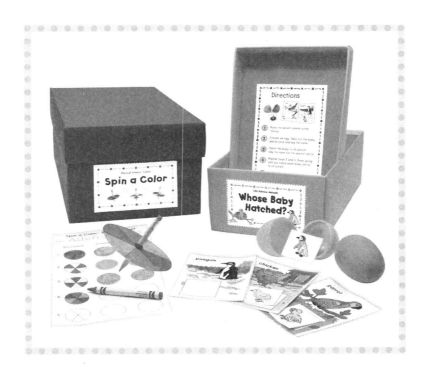

NEW YORK ● TORONTO ● LONDON ● AUCKLAND ● SYDNEY
MEXICO CITY ● NEW DELHI ● HONG KONG ● BUENOS AIRES

Teaching *Resources*

To Alan and Amber

"Stop and consider God's wonders."

JOB 37:14 (NIV)

Cover design by Maria Lilja
Cover photo by Scott Davis
Interior design by Kathy Massaro
Illustrations by Rusty Fletcher and George Ulrich

ISBN: 978-0-439-61652-2

Copyright © 2012 by Immacula A. Rhodes
Illustrations © 2012 by Scholastic Inc.
All rights reserved. Published by Scholastic Inc.
Printed in the U.S.A.

1 2 3 4 5 6 7 8 9 10   40   19 18 17 16 15 14 13 12

CONTENTS

Shoe Box Learning Center	Topic	Page
Life Science		
Critter Sort	Animals	9
Whose Baby Hatched?	Animals	14
The Circle of Life	Life Cycles	19
All About Insects	Insects	21
No Peeking!	The Five Senses (Sight)	23
Listen & Match	The Five Senses (Hearing)	24
Texture Twins	The Five Senses (Touch)	26
Taste Testers	The Five Senses (Taste)	27
Sniff a Whiff	The Five Senses (Smell)	30
Foods to Grow On	Nutrition	32
Be Healthy! Be Safe!	Health and Safety	34
Inside a Seed	Parts of a Seed	37
Plant Power	Plant Growth	39
Living or Not?	Living and Nonliving Things	41
Physical Science		
Does It Stick?	Magnets	44
Will It Sink or Float?	Buoyancy	46
Is It Thirsty?	Absorbency	48
Shadow Show	Light and Shadows	50
Spin a Color	Color Combinations	52
Good Vibrations	Sound	55
Going Up!	Simple Machines	57
What's the Matter?	States of Matter	59
Earth Science		
Signs of the Seasons	Seasons	62
Wonderful Wind	Weather	64
Water Everywhere!	Water Cycle	66
Measuring Weather	Weather Tools	70
In the Sky	Space	72
Moon Prints	Space	75
Ready to Rock!	Rocks	77
Earth's Gifts	Natural Resources	78

About This Book

Convert a simple shoe box into a wonderful world of discovery to bring out the budding scientists in your students! Children come to school with a natural curiosity and love for science. From bug watching, puddle splashing, and rock collecting to shadow chasing, snowflake catching, and noise making, kids engage in concrete explorations and discoveries about the world around them every day. The activities in *Shoe Box Learning Centers: Science* provide hands-on experiences in a ready-to-use format that help children engage in the scientific process while learning key science concepts, skills, and vocabulary.

The 30 portable centers in this book span the life, physical, and earth sciences, with topics that include animal babies, life cycles, the five senses, health and safety, seeds and plants, magnets, light and color, sound, seasons, weather, and more. Each center fits neatly inside a shoe box and can be pulled out as needed and stored conveniently when not in use. When included as part of your science program, these centers help make science concepts concrete and meaningful to children as they investigate, predict, experiment, observe, discover, and share ideas.

Setting Up Shoe Box Learning Centers

The shoe box centers are simple to set up, and most materials required are either included in this book (as reproducible pages) or are already available in the classroom. *Shoe Box Learning Centers: Science* is divided into three sections: Life Science, Physical Science, and Earth Science. The easy-to-follow organization allows you to choose the activities you want to use. Each section includes games and activities that are designed for use by individuals or partners, but can easily be adapted for whole-class lessons or one-on-one teaching. For each center, you'll find:

- **Label and Directions:** The title of each shoe box center becomes the shoe box label—glue it to one side (or end) of the shoe box for easy storage and retrieval. Cut out the student directions and glue to the inside of the lid.

- **Materials:** Check this list to find out which items you'll need for each center. Most materials are readily available, or can be purchased at relatively little expense.

- **Shoe Box Setup:** Here's where you'll find simple directions for assembling each center. In most cases, all you'll need to do is gather materials and make copies of the reproducible pages.

- **Tips:** These ideas include suggestions for introducing the science concept and related vocabulary, background information, prompts to help children make meaningful connections, and helpful hints for making the most of students' learning experiences.

- **Reproducible Pages:** These ready-to-use shoe box center supplies include record sheets, activity mats, game boards, text and picture cards, and patterns.

Tips for Preparing and Using the Centers

Consider the following suggestions as you prepare the centers:

- To make center components (such as activity mats, cards, game boards, and game spinners) sturdier, back them with tagboard and trim to fit. You could also copy them on cardstock.

- For durability, you may want to laminate mats, game boards, text and picture cards, and other materials that will be subject to repeated use. (Laminate game spinners before assembling.)

- When creating a duplicate set of center components as an Answer Key, you might make a color copy of the materials you've already prepared (such as colored animal cards), then follow directions to make the Answer Key.

- Prior to use, thoroughly wash and dry recyclable items, such as spice jars and yogurt containers, and remove labels.

- Store small items, such as game cards and game markers, in resealable plastic bags or envelopes.

- If using plastic shoe boxes, attach the label and directions with wide, clear plastic tape.

- Enlist the help of parent volunteers (or students) to prepare and assemble materials.

- Review the science concept, relevant information and facts, related vocabulary, picture cards, and other materials that will help children build background knowledge, make connections, and better understand the activity.

- To provide support for emerging readers, review text that children will encounter in the activities.

- There's no particular order to follow in teaching with the shoe box centers—simply choose the activities that best support your science curriculum and students' needs.

What the Research Says

An effective early science curriculum encourages children to perform investigations, become objective observers, ask questions, and construct explanations through reasoning and logical thinking. According to the National Science Education Standards, inquiry is central to developing scientific literacy. When learners engage in inquiry, they describe, compare, classify, and communicate their observations. (For more information, go to www.nsta.org/publications/nses.aspx.) Vocabulary development is essential in building the knowledge base needed for learning and understanding science concepts. In fact, the important relationship between vocabulary and reading comprehension extends across all content area subjects. In its review of reading research, the National Reading Panel concluded that effective strategies for building children's vocabulary include direct and indirect instruction, repeated meaningful exposure to new words, and rich and varied contexts for learning. Children learn content area vocabulary best from a combination of teaching methods, including purposeful interaction with the related concepts. The science centers in this book provide rich opportunities to support these learning and literacy goals.

TIP

To help students get the most out of using the shoe box centers, and to facilitate independence, model the activities (including completing record sheets) before inviting children to work with the centers on their own or with partners.

• For long-term storage of the shoe box centers, you may need to dispose of perishable materials—such as the liquids in Taste Testers (page 27), the food-related items in Sniff a Whiff (page 30), and the beans in Inside a Seed (page 37). Refresh those materials when you're ready to use the activities again.

Reinforcing and Assessing Student Learning

One of the greatest benefits of using centers in the classroom is that they provide teachers with the opportunity to work with small groups or individuals on the skills and concepts being taught. The center setup makes it easy to review concepts and provide individual assistance as needed. To record students' progress as they move through the centers, you may want to create an assessment file for each child. To do so, place a copy of the Shoe Box Learning Centers Checklist (page 8) in one side of a pocket folder. In the other pocket, have students store their completed record sheets for review.

For activities that do not require record sheets, sticky notes work well as an assessment tool. Observe and talk with students as they work with a shoe box center. Jot comments on sticky notes and record the child's name, the date, and the shoe box center name. Keep the notes on a separate sheet of paper in the pocket folder for easy reference. In addition, you can record comments for any center on the checklist. Use these assessments to guide students' work with the centers. Encourage them to revisit centers where they show a need for more practice or additional exposure to a science concept.

Bibliography

National Reading Panel. (2000). *Teaching children to read: An evidence-based assessment of the scientific research literature on reading and its implications for reading instruction: Report of the subgroups* (NIH Publication No. 00–4754). Washington, DC: National Institute of Child Health and Human Development.

National Research Council. (1996). *National science education standards: Observe, interact, change, learn.* Washington, DC: National Academy Press.

Meeting the Science Standards

Mid-Continent Research for Education and Learning (McREL), a nationally recognized, nonprofit organization, has compiled and evaluated national and state standards—and proposed what teachers should provide for their students to grow proficient in science, among other curriculum areas. The centers in this book support students in meeting these standards for grades K–2. The following list outlines the standards addressed by the shoe box learning centers, as well as standards related to the nature of science, health, and reading.

Earth and Space Sciences

- Knows that short-term weather conditions can change daily, and weather patterns change over the seasons
- Knows that water can be a liquid or a solid and can change from one form to the other
- Knows that Earth materials consist of solid rocks, soils, water, and gases
- Knows that rocks come in many different shapes and sizes
- Knows vocabulary for major features of the sky
- Knows basic patterns of the Sun and Moon

Life Sciences

- Knows that plants and animals closely resemble their parents
- Knows that differences exist among individuals of the same kind of plant or animal
- Knows that living things and nonliving objects are different
- Knows that living things go through a process of growth and change
- Knows the basic needs of plants and animals

Physical Sciences

- Knows vocabulary used to describe some observable properties of objects
- Sorts objects based on observable properties
- Knows that the physical properties of things can change
- Knows that different objects are made up of many different types of materials and have many different observable properties
- Knows that the Sun supplies heat and light to Earth
- Knows that sound is produced by vibrating objects
- Knows the effects of forces in nature
- Knows that objects can be moved in a number of ways
- Knows that magnets can be used to make some things move without being touched

Nature of Science

- Understands that a model can be used to learn about the real thing
- Uses the senses to make observations
- Records information collected about the physical world
- Uses simple tools to gather information
- Conducts simple investigations to solve a problem or answer a question
- Asks questions about observations
- Develops predictions and explanations
- Understands simple cause-and-effect relationships
- Knows that learning can come from careful observations and simple experiments

Health

- Knows rules for traffic and pedestrian safety
- Knows safe behaviors in the classroom and on the playground
- Knows basic fire, traffic, water, and recreation safety practices
- Knows that some foods are more nutritious than others
- Classifies foods according to the food groups
- Knows basic personal hygiene habits required to maintain health

Source: Kendall, J. S. & Marzano, R. J. (2004). *Content knowledge: A compendium of standards and benchmarks for K–12 education.* Aurora, CO: Mid-continent Research for Education and Learning. Online database: http://www.mcrel.org/standards-benchmarks/

Shoe Box Learning Centers Checklist

Name _____

Shoe Box Learning Center	Date	Comments
Critter Sort		
Whose Baby Hatched?		
The Circle of Life		
All About Insects		
No Peeking!		
Listen & Match		
Texture Twins		
Taste Testers		
Sniff a Whiff		
Foods to Grow On		
Be Healthy! Be Safe!		
Inside a Seed		
Plant Power		
Living or Not?		
Does It Stick?		
Will It Sink or Float?		
Is It Thirsty?		
Shadow Show		
Spin a Color		
Good Vibrations		
Going Up!		
What's the Matter?		
Signs of the Seasons		
Wonderful Wind		
Water Everywhere!		
Measuring Weather		
In the Sky		
Moon Prints		
Ready to Rock!		
Earth's Gifts		

Critter Sort

Children sort animals to show understanding of the characteristics of different animal groups.

Materials

- shoe box
- box label
- student directions
- animal-group mats (pages 10–12)
- answer key (page 12)
- animal cards (page 13)

Shoe Box Setup

Copy, color, and cut apart the animal-group mats and animal cards. Cut out the answer key. Then place the mats, animal cards, and answer key in the shoe box. Glue the label to one end of the box and the student directions to the inside of the lid.

TIPS

- To introduce this center, discuss the characteristics of the five animal groups: amphibians, birds, fish, mammals, and reptiles. You might use the lists on the animal mats, sharing other characteristics as desired. Invite children to name animals that belong to each group and tell why they belong.

- As you model how to complete the center activity, review the list of characteristics on each animal-group mat and name the animal on each card.

- As children complete the activity, encourage them to note common characteristics among animals that belong to the same group. For example, the crocodile and turtle have scaly skin, the hummingbird and turkey have feathers and lay eggs.

Life Science: Animals

Critter Sort

Directions

(1) Place the animal cards faceup.

(2) Choose a mat and name the animal group. Read the characteristics of animals in that group.

(3) Find each animal that belongs to the group. Name the animal and place it on the mat.

(4) Repeat steps 2 and 3 for the other animal groups. Keep going until you match each animal to its group.

(5) Use the Answer Key to check your work.

Amphibians

Most amphibians:

- have smooth skin

- are born with gills and develop lungs later

- can live on land and in water

- lay eggs in water

Birds

Most birds:

- have feathers

- have wings and can fly

- lay eggs

- build nests for their eggs

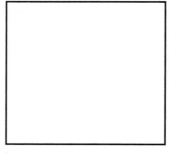

Fish

Most fish:

- have scaly skin

- live in water

- have fins that help them swim

- breathe through gills

Mammals

Most mammals:

- grow fur or hair

- breathe through lungs

- give birth to live babies

- make milk to feed their babies

Reptiles

Most reptiles:

- have dry, scaly skin

- breathe through lungs

- lay eggs on land

- have babies that look like the parents

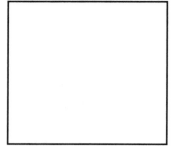

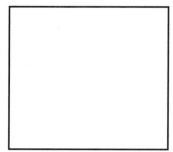

Answer Key

Amphibians	Birds	Fish	Mammals	Reptiles
frog	duck	goldfish	elephant	crocodile
salamander	eagle	seahorse	pig	iguana
tadpole	hummingbird	shark	squirrel	snake
toad	pelican	swordfish	tiger	turtle

Critter Sort ● Animal Cards

frog	toad	salamander	tadpole
duck	eagle	hummingbird	pelican
goldfish	shark	swordfish	seahorse
pig	tiger	elephant	squirrel
snake	iguana	crocodile	turtle

Shoe Box Learning Centers: Science © 2012 by Immacula A. Rhodes, Scholastic Teaching Resources

Whose Baby Hatched?

Children "hatch" baby animals to explore how offspring resemble their parents at birth and how they will change as they mature.

Materials

- shoe box
- box label
- student directions
- parent animal cards (pages 15–17)
- baby animal cards (page 18)
- 12 plastic eggs
- answer key (see Shoe Box Setup)
- page-protector sleeves

Shoe Box Setup

Copy the parent and baby animal cards. Color the animal cards (using reference such as photos from informational texts and online resources), then cut them apart. Place each baby animal card in an egg. To make the answer key, copy an extra set of parent and baby animal cards. Cut apart only the baby animal cards and glue each next to its parent. Slip the answer-key pages into page-protector sleeves. Place the parent animal cards, eggs, and answer key in the shoe box. Glue the label to one end of the box and the student directions to the inside of the lid.

○ ○ ○ TIPS ○ ○ ○

- Share a nonfiction text about animals that lay eggs, such as *Chickens Aren't the Only Ones* by Ruth Heller (Grosset & Dunlap, 1981).
- Point out that while bird eggs are usually hard, reptile eggs are sometimes leathery. Also, all birds hatch from eggs, but some reptiles give birth to live young.
- As you introduce the center, review the name for each baby and parent animal. As students complete the activity, prompt them to describe how baby animals resemble their parents at birth and how they will change as they mature.

Life Science: Animals

Whose Baby Hatched?

Directions

1. Place the parent animal cards faceup.

2. Choose an egg. Take out the baby animal card and say the name.

3. Match the baby to its parent. Say the name for the parent animal.

4. Repeat steps 2 and 3. Keep going until you match each baby animal to its parent.

5. Use the Answer Key to check your work.

chicken

owl

parrot

peacock

penguin

robin

ostrich

duck

alligator

lizard

snake

turtle

chick (chicken)   owlet (owl)   chick (parrot)   peachick or chick (peacock)

chick (penguin)   chick (robin)   chick (ostrich)   duckling (duck)

hatchling (alligator)   hatchling (lizard)   hatchling (snake)   hatchling (turtle)

Shoe Box Learning Centers: Science © 2012 by Immacula A. Rhodes, Scholastic Teaching Resources

The Circle of Life

Children sequence the developmental stages of a frog and butterfly to show understanding of life cycles.

Materials

- shoe box
- box label
- student directions
- life-cycle cards and animal circles (page 20)
- two 6-inch sturdy paper plates
- permanent marker
- ten wood, spring-type clothespins
- paper
- crayons

Shoe Box Setup

Copy, color, and cut out the life-cycle cards and animal circles. Glue each circle to a plate and number the rim clockwise from 1–5, spacing the numbers evenly. Glue each life-cycle card to a clothespin. For self-checking purposes, label the back of each set of clothespins 1–5 in the order of the animal's life stages. Place the animal plates, life-cycle cards/clothespins, paper, and crayons in the shoe box. Glue the label to one end of the box and the student directions to the inside of the lid.

TIPS

- Share *From Tadpole to Frog* by Wendy Pfeffer (HarperCollins, 1994) and *From Caterpillar to Butterfly* by Deborah Heiligman (HarperCollins, 1996), or other similar books. Discuss the life cycle of each animal and review related vocabulary, such as *metamorphosis, tadpole, froglet, molting,* and *chrysalis.*

- As you model the center, think aloud about the life stage represented on each card. Have children complete the center activity with partners. Encourage them to describe their animal's life cycle and share what they know about each stage.

The Circle of Life

Directions
(For partners)

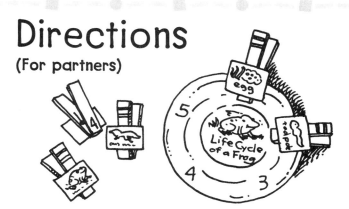

1. Each partner chooses an animal plate.

2. Find the cards for your animal.

3. Clip each card on the plate in order to show the life cycle. Check the back of the clothespin if you need help.

4. Tell your partner about your animal's life cycle. Use the animal plate to help you.

5. Remove the cards. Switch plates with your partner, then repeat steps 2 through 4.

6. Choose one of the animals. On a sheet of paper, draw your own pictures to show the life cycle of the animal.

The Circle of Life

Life-Cycle Cards and Animal Circles

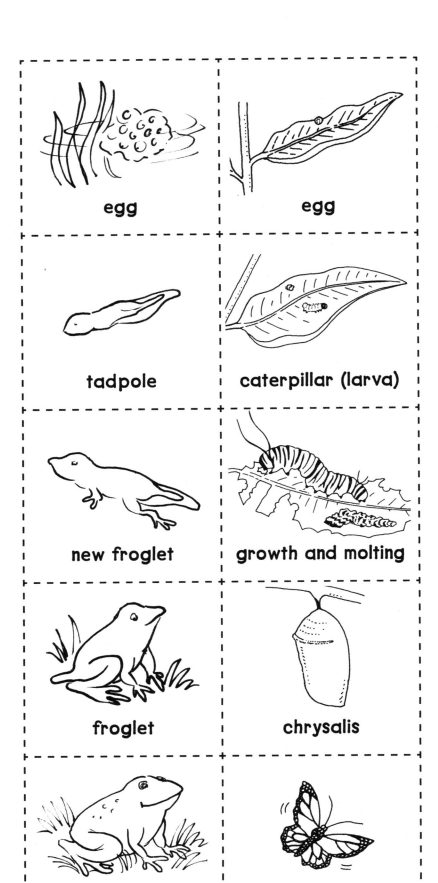

egg	egg
tadpole	caterpillar (larva)
new froglet	growth and molting
froglet	chrysalis
adult frog	adult butterfly

Life Cycle of a Frog

Life Cycle of a Butterfly

Shoe Box Learning Centers: Science
© 2012 by Immacula A. Rhodes, Scholastic Teaching Resources

All About Insects

Children create their own insects to demonstrate understanding of the characteristics of these animals.

Materials

- shoe box
- box label
- student directions
- insect cards (page 22)
- paper
- crayons
- assorted craft materials (for insect models)
- student scissors
- glue

Shoe Box Setup

Copy, color, and cut apart the insect cards. Gather a supply of insect-making craft materials, such as craft sticks, foam peanuts, pipe cleaners, tissue paper, yarn, fabric and felt scraps, textured papers, wiggle eyes, fast-drying modeling clay, plastic bottle caps, and toothpicks. Place the insect cards, craft supplies (restocking as needed), paper, and crayons in the shoe box. Glue the label to one end of the box and the student directions to the inside of the lid.

TIPS

- Share *Bugs Are Insects* by Anne Rockwell (HarperCollins, 2001), or a similar book. Discuss features that make insects different from other "creepy crawly" animals, such as spiders and scorpions.
- Use the insect cards to review characteristics of insects: head, thorax, abdomen, and six legs. Explain that most, but not all, insects also have antennae and two pairs of wings.

Life Science: Insects

All About Insects

Directions
(For partners)

1. Look at the insect cards. Read the name of each body part.

2. On a piece of paper, draw your own insect and label the parts.

3. Choose materials to create a model of your insect. You will need to make the head, thorax, abdomen, and legs.

4. Does your insect have antennae and wings? If it does, choose materials for these parts, too.

5. Put your insect together.

6. Tell your partner about your insect. Name each body part. Find the same body part on an insect card.

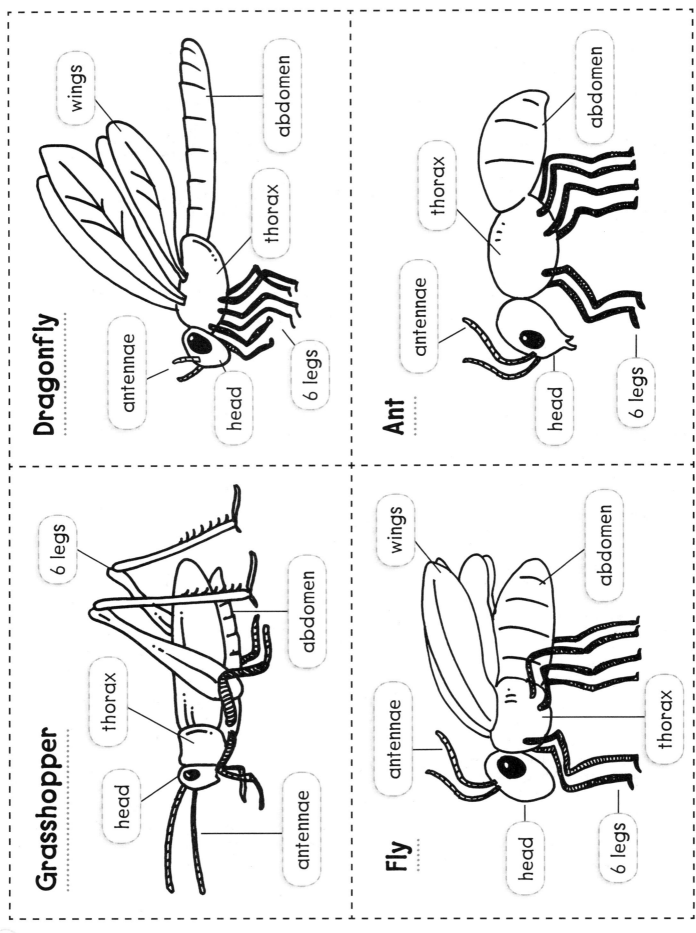

Dragonfly

wings

abdomen

thorax

antennae

head

6 legs

Ant

thorax

abdomen

antennae

head

6 legs

Grasshopper

6 legs

thorax

abdomen

head

antennae

Fly

wings

abdomen

antennae

thorax

head

6 legs

Shoe Box Learning Centers: Science © 2012 by Immacula A. Rhodes, Scholastic Teaching Resources

No Peeking!

As children try to complete a task without looking, they discover how the sense of sight helps them learn about their world.

Materials

- shoe box
- box label
- student directions
- response sheets (see Shoe Box Setup)
- ten 1-inch wooden cubes
- half-sheets of plain paper
- crayons

Shoe Box Setup

To create student response sheets, label the top of a sheet of paper (half- or whole sheet) with the sentence starter: *I use sight when I ___.* Copy to make a class supply. Place response sheets, cubes, paper, and crayons in the shoe box. Glue the label to one end of the box and the student directions to the inside of the lid.

TIPS

- Share *The Sense of Sight* by Ellen Weiss (Children's Press, 2009), or a similar book.

- Have children close their eyes, then hold up an object for them to identify. Did they guess correctly? Discuss how students use sight to explore and learn about their surroundings.

- Explain how the sense of sight works: Light rays from an object pass through to the back of the eye. There, a special nerve helps the brain process the image and then send a message about what the person is seeing.

Life Science: The Five Senses (Sight)

No Peeking!

Directions
(For partners)

1. Take turns with your partner doing each activity two times. Keep your eyes open the first time. Then close your eyes and repeat the activity. (No peeking!)

   - Build a tower with the cubes.
   - Build a pyramid with the cubes.
   - Draw a happy face on a sheet of paper.

2. Discuss with your partner which way was easier: with sight or without sight 〰〰 .

3. Complete a response sheet. Draw and label three ways you use sight.

Listen & Match

Children explore hearing as they match sounds and identify items that make the sounds.

Materials

- shoe box
- box label
- student directions
- sound mats (page 25)
- 12 identical, opaque plastic mint containers (with flip-up tops)
- small items to use as noisemakers (such as uncooked rice, dried beans, pennies, paper clips, pompoms, jingle bells)
- sticker dots in six colors
- six resealable snack-size plastic bags

Shoe Box Setup

Place the "noisemaker" items in the containers, creating a pair of each. For self-checking purposes, affix the same color sticker dot to the bottom of each pair of containers. Use a separate color for each sound. Copy and cut out six sound mats and fill in the name of an item on each. Place a few of each noisemaker item in a bag. Seal the bags, then staple each bag to the bottom of the corresponding mat as indicated. Place the shakers and sound mats in the shoe box. Glue the label to one end of the box and the student directions to the inside of the lid.

TIPS

- Brainstorm a list of sounds and their sources (i.e., "bang," drum or "moo," cow).
- Explain how the sense of hearing works: When a sound is made, sound waves travel deep into the ear, causing the eardrum and three small bones in the inner ear to vibrate. There, nerves send a message to the brain, which lets the listener know what the sound is and what made it.

24

Life Science: The Five Senses (Hearing)

Listen & Match

Directions
(For partners)

1. Place the shakers in three rows of four shakers each.

2. Take turns choosing two shakers. Shake each one and listen.

3. Do they make the same sound?
   - Check the colors on the bottom. If they match, go to step 4.
   - If they do not match, put the shakers back.

4. What do you think makes the sound? Put the shakers on that mat.

5. When the activity ends, look inside a shaker on each mat to check your answers.

Listen & Match

I think I hear _____

in the shakers.

[Staple bag here.]

Listen & Match

I think I hear _____

in the shakers.

[Staple bag here.]

Texture Twins

Children use their sense of touch to explore and match a variety of textures.

Materials

- shoe box
- box label
- student directions
- cardboard
- eight differently textured materials (such as sandpaper, craft foam, craft fur, felt, corrugated paper, grip shelf liner, sponge, bubble wrap)
- craft glue
- brown paper lunch bag
- plain index cards

Shoe Box Setup

Cut the cardboard into 16 disks (each 3 inches in diameter). From each textured material, cut three circles (each 3 inches in diameter). Glue each set of textured circles to the disks as follows: Glue two same-textured circles to each side of one disk (to make it two-sided). Glue the remaining textured circle to a second disk. After the glue dries, place all two-sided disks in the bag. Next, write words that describe the textures—such as *soft*, *smooth*, and *bumpy*—on index cards (one word per card). Place the bag of two-sided disks, the single-sided disks, and the word cards in the shoe box. Glue the label to one end of the box and the student directions to the inside of the lid.

° ° ° TIPS ° ° °

- Tell children that their sense of touch gives information about how things feel, such as soft or hard, rough or smooth, hot or cold, and wet or dry. Invite them to feel and describe different textures.

- Explain how the sense of touch works: The skin that covers our body is filled with nerves. When we touch something, these nerves send a message to the brain, which gives us information about how the object feels. Touch also lets us feel pain and temperature as a way to protect us.

Life Science: The Five Senses (Touch)

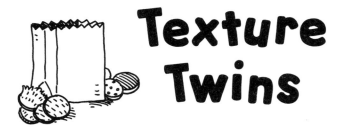

Texture Twins

Directions
(For partners)

(1) Partner 1 gives Partner 2 a one-sided disk.

(2) Partner 2 follows these directions:

- Feel the texture of your disk.
- Use your sense of touch to find the matching disk in the bag.
- Take out the disk and compare.
- If the disk matches, describe the texture. Use the word cards to help you.
- If the disk doesn't match, try again.

(3) Repeat steps 1 and 2 with each one-sided disk.

(4) Place the two-sided disks back in the bag. Trade places and repeat the activity.

Taste Testers

Children explore the four basic tastes and identify foods for each one.

Materials

- shoe box
- box label
- student directions
- taste mat and food cards (page 28)
- record sheet (page 29)
- four 2-ounce spray bottles, with caps
- clear liquids (dissolve dry ingredients):
  - sour: $\frac{1}{4}$ cup vinegar
  - salty: $\frac{1}{4}$ cup water + $\frac{1}{2}$ tsp. sea salt
  - bitter: $\frac{1}{4}$ cup water + $\frac{1}{4}$ tsp. aluminum-free baking powder
  - sweet: $\frac{1}{4}$ cup water + 1 tsp. sugar
- sticker dots labeled 1–4
- plastic spoons (one per child)
- paper towels

Shoe Box Setup

Copy and cut out four taste mats, one set of food cards, and a supply of record sheets. Affix a numbered sticker dot to each bottle. Pour the liquids in the numbered bottles as follows: 1–sour, 2–salty, 3–bitter, and 4–sweet. For self-checking purposes, fill in a spray-bottle number on each mat and label the back with the corresponding taste. Also, label the back of each food card with the number for that taste. Place the taste mats, food cards, record sheets, spray bottles, plastic spoons, and paper towels in the shoe box. Glue the label to one end of the box and the student directions to the inside of the lid.

TIPS

- Explain how the sense of taste works: The tongue is covered with taste buds that are filled with nerves. When you eat something, the nerves send messages about how the food tastes to the brain. The brain then lets you know if the food is bitter, salty, sour, or sweet (the four basic tastes).

- Brainstorm a list of foods that belong to the four taste categories.

- Have students prepare the taste samples over a sink, if possible.

Life Science: The Five Senses (Taste)

Taste Testers

Directions

1. Place each spray bottle next to the mat with the matching number. Take a spoon and paper towel.

2. Spray a few drops from spray bottle 1 onto the spoon. Taste.

3. What is the taste: bitter, salty, sour, or sweet? Check the back of mat 1 to see if you are correct. Place the spray bottle on that taste.

4. Dry your spoon. Repeat steps 2 and 3 for each spray bottle. Then throw away your spoon.

5. Match the food cards to the mats. Check your answers on the back of the cards.

6. Complete a record sheet.

Taste Testers: Bottle _____

| bitter | salty | sour | sweet |

Three foods
that have
this taste:

| | | |

Bitter	**Salty**	**Sour**	**Sweet**
 coffee	 pretzel	pickles	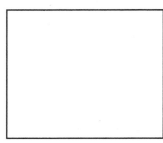 apple
 orange peel	 chips	 yogurt	raisins
 spinach	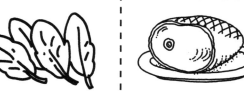 ham	lime	cookie

Shoe Box Learning Centers: Science © 2012 by Immacula A. Rhodes, Scholastic Teaching Resources

Taste Testers: Record Sheet

Name_____ Date_____

Color the picture for your answer.	Taste	Draw two foods for each taste.
I 😊 😝 this taste.	bitter	
I 😊 😝 this taste.	salty	
I 😊 😝 this taste.	sour	
I 😊 😝 this taste.	sweet	

Sniff a Whiff

Children use their sense of smell to identify mystery scents.

Materials

- shoe box
- box label
- student directions
- sorting mat (page 31)
- six plastic spice jars with flip-up lids
- sticker dots labeled 1–6
- fragrant items (cinnamon stick, coffee beans, dehydrated onion, dehydrated lemon peel, cedar shavings, broken pieces of peppermint candy)
- six 4-inch gauze squares (single layer)
- half-sheets of plain paper
- crayons

Shoe Box Setup

Copy and color the sorting mat. To make self-checking scent jars, affix a numbered sticker dot to the bottom of each jar. Next, wrap each scented item in a gauze square, and place each one in the jar labeled with the number that corresponds to that scent (as indicated on the mat). Then place the jars, scent sorting mat, paper, and crayons in the shoe box. Glue the label to one end of the box and the student directions to the inside of the lid.

∘ ° ∘ TIPS ∘ ° ∘

- Read and discuss *The Sense of Smell* by Ellen Weiss (Children's Press, 2009), or a similar book. Brainstorm a list of things that have a scent.

- Explain how smell works: Invisible particles from a scent float through the air and into the nose. Tiny smell cells in the nasal passages send a message about the scent to the olfactory nerve, which then sends the information to the brain. The brain, in turn, tells you about the smell.

- Point out that the sense of smell can bring pleasure (the scent of fresh-baked brownies) as well as warn of danger (the odor of smoke from a fire).

Life Science: The Five Senses (Smell)

Sniff a Whiff

Directions

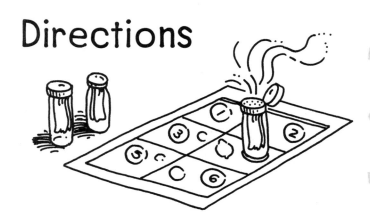

1 Place the sorting mat faceup.

2 Choose a jar. Flip open the lid and smell. What scent do you smell?

3 Find that picture and number on the mat. Place the jar on that number.

4 Repeat steps 2 and 3. Keep going until you match each jar to a picture on the mat.

5 Check your work by looking at the numbers on the bottom of the jars.

6 Use the paper to draw three things you like to smell.

Sniff a Whiff

1

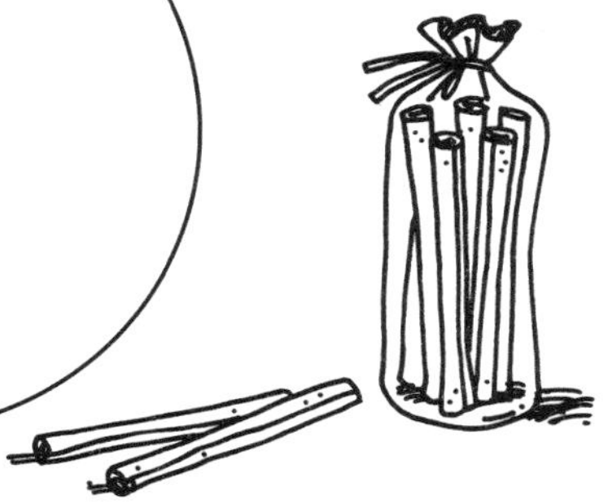

cinnamon

2

coffee

3

onion

4

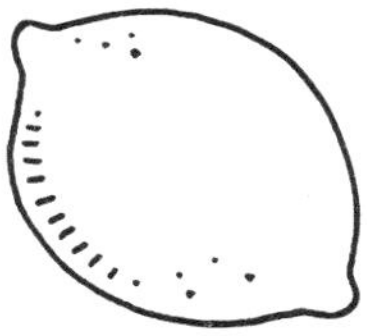

lemon

5

cedar

6

peppermint

Foods to Grow On

Children develop an awareness of good nutrition as they sort foods into the main five food groups.

Materials

- shoe box
- box label
- student directions
- food cards (page 33)
- six 6-inch paper plates
- five 4- by 6-inch plain index cards
- response sheets (see Shoe Box Setup)
- crayons

Shoe Box Setup

Copy, color, and cut out the food cards. For self-checking purposes, sort the cards by food groups and label the back of each card with the corresponding group (fruits, grains, protein, vegetables, dairy). Label a long edge of each index card with a food group. Glue each index card to the bottom of a plate so that the food group label extends beyond the plate and is easily visible. (See illustration in the student directions.) To create a response sheet, trace the remaining plate on plain paper, write "My Healthy Foods" across the top, then copy a class supply. Place the food cards, labeled plates, response sheets, and crayons in the shoe box. Glue the label to one end of the box and the student directions to the inside of the lid.

TIPS

- Share *Good Enough to Eat* by Lizzy Rockwell (HarperCollins, 2009), or a similar book. Then name the five main food groups: *fruits*, *grains*, *protein*, *vegetables*, and *dairy*. Compile a list of foods that belong to each group.

- Review the food cards with students before they complete the center activity.

Life Science: Nutrition

Foods to Grow On

Directions

1. Place the food cards faceup. Line up the plates.

2. Pick a card and name the food. What food group does it belong to?

3. Check your answer on the back of the card. Then place the card on the matching plate.

4. Repeat steps 2 and 3 to match each food card to a plate.

5. Complete a My Healthy Foods sheet. Draw healthy foods from each food group on the "plate."

apple	bananas	pear	grapes
cereal	crackers	bread	rice
almonds	chicken	egg	fish
broccoli	carrots	peas	corn
cheese	milk	yogurt	soy milk

Be Healthy! Be Safe!

Children explore health and safety practices as they play an adapted version of tic-tac-toe.

Materials

- shoe box
- box label
- student directions
- game boards and game cards (pages 35–36)
- answer key (see Shoe Box Setup)
- page-protector sleeves

Shoe Box Setup

Copy, color, and cut apart the game boards and game cards. To create an answer key, duplicate and prepare another set of these components. Next, glue each text card to the corresponding box on the game board. Slip the game cards back-to-back in a page-protector sleeve. Place the game boards, game cards, and answer key in the shoe box. Glue the label to one end of the box and the student directions to the inside of the lid.

○ ○ ○ TIPS ○ ○ ○

- Engage students in a discussion about ways that they stay healthy, such as washing their hands and choosing healthy foods.

- Continue the discussion, focusing this time on safety practices, such as wearing a helmet when riding a bike, reading and following signs, and calling 9-1-1 in an emergency. Invite children to share other safety practices and explain how each one helps keep them safe.

- To introduce children to the health and safety practices featured in the center activity, review the text cards and pictures on the game boards.

Life Science: Health & Safety

Be Healthy! Be Safe!

Directions
(For 2 players)

1. Each player chooses a game board ("Be Healthy!" or "Be Safe!"). Shuffle the cards. Stack them facedown.

2. Players take turns following these steps:
   - Take the top card.
   - Read the card.
   - Does it match a picture on your board? If so, cover the picture with the card. If not, place the card at the bottom of the stack.

3. The first player to cover three boxes in a row wins that round.

4. Use the Answer Key to check the winner's game board.

5. Play two more rounds. Start over each time.

Be Healthy!

Visit the doctor.

Take a bath.

Get fresh air.

Brush your teeth.

Wash your hands.

Get enough rest.

Eat healthy foods.

Visit the dentist.

Exercise every day.

Be Safe!

Never
play with
matches.

Wear a seatbelt.	Walk when indoors.	Read the signs.	Put on sunscreen.
Stop, drop, and roll.	Call 9-1-1.	Look both ways.	Wear a helmet.

Inside a Seed

As children examine the inside of a seed, they develop understanding of how the different parts help it grow into a plant.

Materials

- shoe box
- box label
- student directions
- seed diagram and seed labels (page 38)
- large, dried lima beans (soaked in water overnight)
- small plastic lids (as from a yogurt or sour cream container; one per child)
- quick-drying clay
- tissue paper
- yarn (cut into $\frac{1}{2}$-inch lengths)
- flat toothpicks
- paper
- student scissors
- glue

Shoe Box Setup

Make one copy of the seed diagram, then copy a supply of the seed labels. If desired, make a seed model from the craft items for children to use as reference in making their own. Place the diagram, seed labels, beans (in a plastic bag), seed model, plastic lids, clay, tissue paper, yarn, toothpicks, paper, scissors, and glue in the shoe box. Glue the label to one end of the box and the student directions to the inside of the lid.

TIPS

- Explain that a seed has everything it needs to grow into a plant. Using the diagram, review the parts of a seed.
- Explain that the *coat* covers the outside of the seed and provides protection. The *embryo* is a baby plant that has a tiny root and leaves. The *food storage* nourishes the baby plant in its early stages of growth.
- Soak the beans in blue-tinted water to help make the embryo more visible. Demonstrate how to gently pry open the pre-soaked bean (seed) to expose its interior.

Life Science: Parts of a Seed

Inside a Seed

Directions
(For partners)

1. Look at the seed diagram together with your partner. Name each part.

2. Open a seed and find each part.

3. Now each of you will make your own seed. Use the items below:
   - plastic lid (coat)
   - clay (food storage)
   - torn tissue paper (leaves)
   - yarn (root)

4. Glue the seed you made to a sheet of paper. Then cut out a set of labels. Glue each label to a toothpick.

5. Add the labels to your seed.

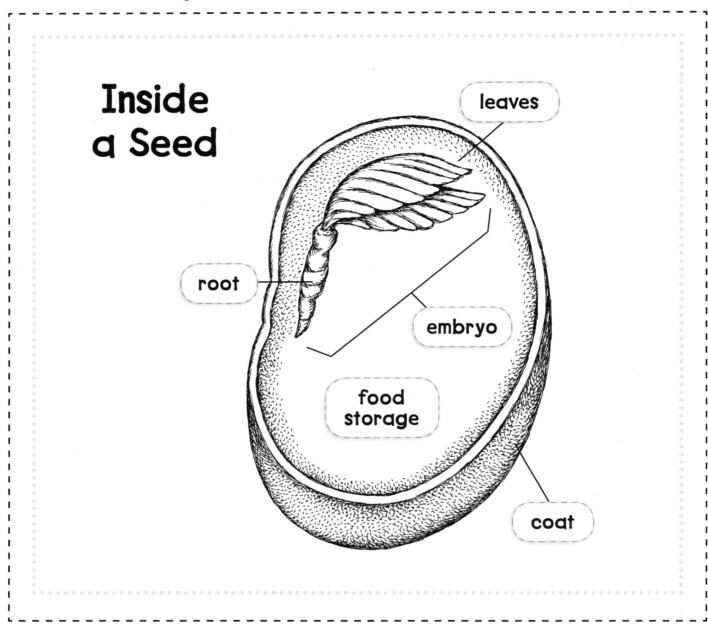

Inside a Seed

leaves

root

embryo

food storage

coat

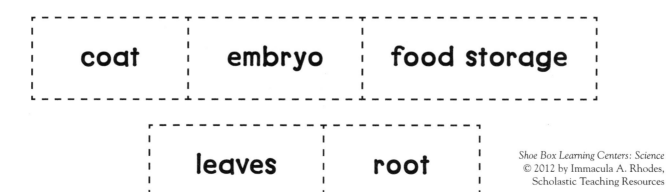

coat | embryo | food storage

leaves | root

Shoe Box Learning Centers: Science
© 2012 by Immacula A. Rhodes,
Scholastic Teaching Resources

Plant Power

Children assemble a flower as they learn about plant needs and their parts.

Materials

- shoe box
- box label
- student directions
- activity mat, picture cards, and word labels (page 40)
- answer key (see Shoe Box Setup)
- sandpaper (cut to $\frac{1}{2}$ by 7 inches)
- small, artificial daisy on stem
- page-protector sleeve
- paper
- crayons

Shoe Box Setup

Copy and cut apart the activity mat, word labels, and picture cards. Color the picture cards. To create an answer key, prepare a duplicate set of these components. Next, glue the picture cards to the mat, draw a plant that resembles the one used for the activity, and glue each label next to its corresponding plant part. Glue the sandpaper to the mat where indicated and trim to size. Then, separate the daisy into four parts: the flower, a 5-inch stem, and two leaves. *Note: If the artificial stem has wire in it, wrap it with floral tape to blunt any sharp ends.* Slip the answer key into a page-protector sleeve. Place the activity mat, word labels, picture cards, answer key, daisy parts, paper, and crayons in the shoe box. Glue the label to one end of the box and the student directions to the inside of the lid.

TIPS

- Share *From Seed to Plant* by Gail Gibbons (Holiday House, 1993), or a similar book.
- Review these parts of a plant: roots, stem, leaves, flower. Discuss a plant's need for soil, water, and sun. Explain that most plants require all three to grow. You might share that plants also need air.

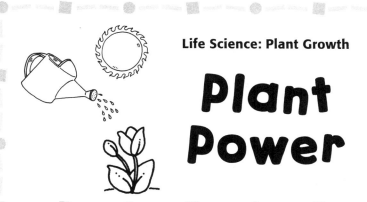

Life Science: Plant Growth

Plant Power

Directions

1. Place the mat, picture cards, and word labels faceup. Take out the plant parts.

2. What does a plant need to grow? Match the picture cards to each need.

3. Put the plant parts together. Build the plant from the soil up.

4. Name each part. Match the word labels to the parts.

5. Use the Answer Key to check your work.

6. Draw your own plant, and label the parts. Write three things plants need to grow.

Plant Power

Plant Needs

Plant Parts

sun

water

soil

Glue sandpaper here.

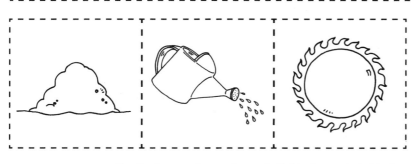

Shoe Box Learning Centers: Science © 2012 by Immacula A. Rhodes,
Scholastic Teaching Resources

flower

leaves

stem

roots

Living or Not?

Children play a game to identify and compare living and nonliving things.

Materials

- shoe box
- box label
- student directions
- game board (page 42)
- spinner, game markers, and answer key (page 43)
- brass fastener
- paper clip

Shoe Box Setup

Copy, color, and cut out the game board, spinner, and game markers. Also, copy and cut out the answer key. Assemble the spinner and fold the game markers, as shown on page 43. Place the game board, spinner, markers, and answer key in the shoe box. Glue the label to one end of the box and the student directions to the inside of the lid.

TIPS

- To introduce the concept of living and nonliving things, share *What's Alive?* by Kathleen Weidner Zoehfeld (HarperCollins, 1995), or a similar book.

- Point out that living things eat, grow, need water, and reproduce (have "babies"). Most also move and need air. Explain how a dog, plant, and fish meet the criteria of a living thing. Then discuss how a rock, book, and pencil are nonliving things.

- On chart paper, list in random order a variety of living and nonliving things. Have children tell whether each item is living or nonliving and explain their thinking.

Life Science: Living & Nonliving Things

Living or Not?

Directions
(For 2 players)

1 Each player places a game marker on **Start**.

2 Take turns spinning the spinner. Did it land on **Living** or **Nonliving**?

3 Move your marker to the next space that shows that kind of thing. Tell why it is living or nonliving.

4 Check the Answer Key.
- If correct, stay on the space.
- If not, move back to where you were.

5 Keep taking turns. The first one to reach **Finish** wins the game.

Living or Not?

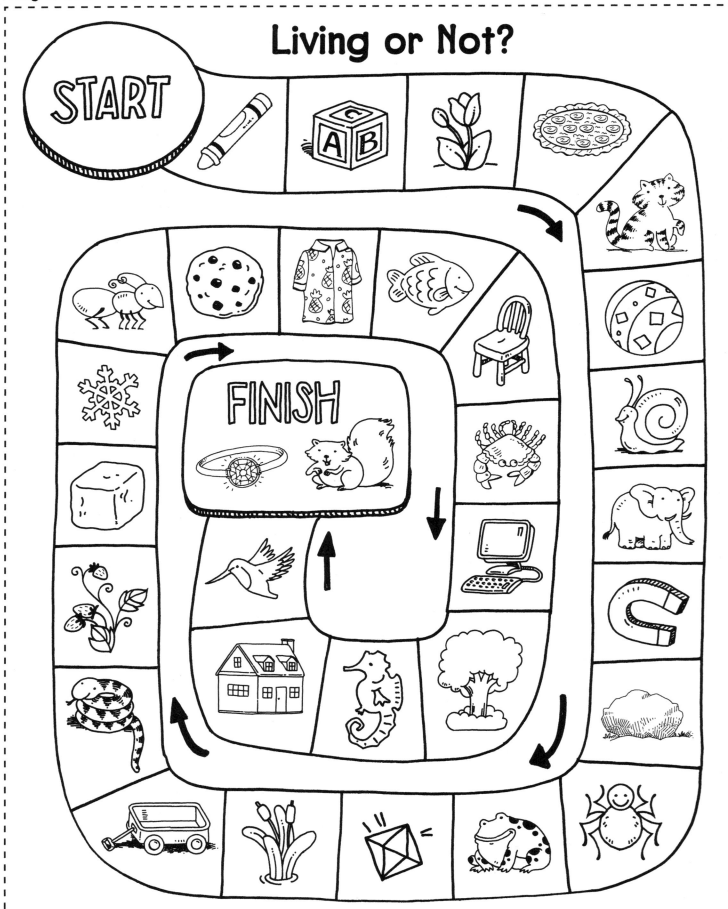

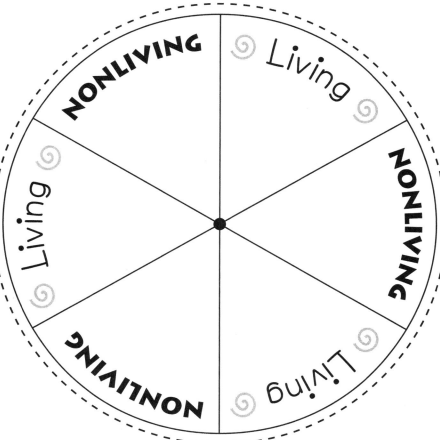

Fold here.

Fold here.

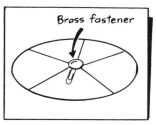

Brass fastener

Assemble the spinner using a paper clip and brass fastener as shown. Make sure the paper clip spins easily.

Living or Not? Answer Key

Living Things

 flower

 strawberries

 cat

 ant

 snail

 goldfish

 elephant

 crab

 spider

 tree

 frog

 seahorse

 plant

 hummingbird

 snake

 squirrel

Nonliving Things

 crayon

 ice cube

 block

 snowflake

 pizza

cookie

magnet

shirt

rock

chair

jewel

computer

 wagon

 house

ring

Does It Stick?

Children explore the magnetic attraction of a variety of materials.

Materials

- shoe box
- box label
- student directions
- activity mat (page 45)
- record sheets (see Shoe Box Setup)
- strong magnet
- small, magnetic objects (such as a paper clip, metal spoon, binder clip, flat washer, flat-bottom screw, key ring, and jingle bell)
- small, nonmagnetic objects (such as a plastic counter, penny, rubber band, ball of foil, cardboard puzzle piece, key, craft stick, and foam shape)

Shoe Box Setup

Make three copies of the activity mat. Fill in "Predictions" on one copy (My Predictions), "Results" (My Results) on another, and "Record Sheet" (My Record Sheet) on the third. Laminate the Predictions and Results mats. Copy a class set of the record sheet version. Place the activity mats, magnet, magnetic and nonmagnetic objects, record sheets, and crayons in the shoe box. Glue the label to one end of the box and the student directions to the inside of the lid.

° ° ° TIPS ° ° °

- Read *What Makes a Magnet?* by Franklyn M. Branley (HarperCollins, 1996), or a similar book.
- Explain that magnets have an invisible force that attracts metals. Help students understand that not all metal objects are magnetic. A paper clip made of steel wire is magnetic. A penny is not. Paper, plastic, rubber, glass, and wood are also not magnetic.

Physical Science: Magnets

Does It Stick?

Directions
(For partners)

1. Take out the activity mats and objects. Place the magnet to the side.

2. Choose an object with your partner.
   - Predict: Will it stick to the magnet?
   - Decide with your partner.
   - Then place the object under No or Yes on the My Predictions mat.

3. Repeat step 2 with each object.

4. Use the magnet to test each object. Did it stick? Move the object to the My Results mat under No or Yes.

5. Complete a record sheet. Draw and label objects that are not magnetic (No) and that are magnetic (Yes).

Does It Stick? My _____

| No | Yes |

Shoe Box Learning Centers: Science © 2012 by Immacula A. Rhodes, Scholastic Teaching Resources

Will It Sink or Float?

Children explore buoyancy as they predict and test whether objects sink or float.

Materials

- plastic shoe box with removable lid
- box label
- student directions
- wide, clear packing tape
- activity mat (page 47)
- record sheet (see Shoe Box Setup)
- small objects that float (such as a cork, craft stick, foam shape, ping pong ball)
- small objects that sink (such as a key, penny, solid rubber ball, rock)
- crayons

Shoe Box Setup

Make three copies of the activity mat. Fill in the label at the top as follows: "Predictions," "Results," and "Record Sheet." Laminate the Predictions and Results mats, and copy a class supply of record sheets. Note that students will place water in the plastic shoe box to perform the activity. Mark a water line about one-third from the top as a guide. Place the activity mats, record sheets, and objects in the shoe box. Tape the label (covering it with clear packing tape) to one end of the box and the student directions to the inside of the lid.

° ° ° TIPS ° ° °

- Teach the words *buoyant* and *buoyancy*:

  An object that floats is buoyant; *it stays on top of water. When an object is placed in water, its weight pushes down on the water while the water pushes up against the object. If the water pushes up more than the object pushes down, the object will float. If the object pushes down more, the object will sink.*

- Reinforce using the water line on the shoe box as a guide for filling it with water.

- After completing the activity, remind students to empty and dry the shoe box before returning the materials.

Physical Science: Buoyancy

Will It Sink or Float?

Directions
(For partners)

1. Empty the shoe box.

2. Fill the box with water up to the line.

3. Choose an object. Predict: Will it float or sink? Decide with your partner.

4. Place the object on the Predictions mat to show your answer.

5. Repeat steps 3 and 4 with each object. Keep going until you use all of the objects.

6. Now test each object. Does it float or sink? Dry the object. Then place it on the Results mat.

7. Draw your results on a record sheet.

Will It Sink or Float? _____

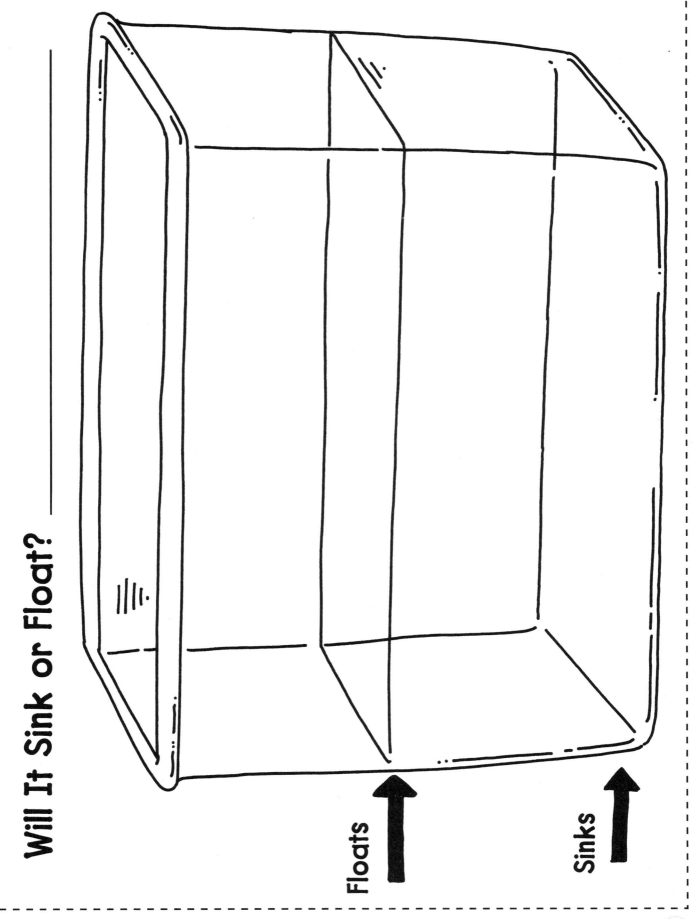

Floats

Sinks

Shoe Box Learning Centers: Science © 2012 by Immacula A. Rhodes, Scholastic Teaching Resources

Is It Thirsty?

Children explore the ability of different materials to absorb or repel liquids.

Materials

- shoe box
- box label
- student directions
- record sheet (page 49)
- two plastic lids (such as from large yogurt containers)
- permanent marker
- sponge, newspaper, page-protector sleeve, cotton fabric, foil, waxed paper (each cut into a supply of $1\frac{1}{2}$-inch squares)
- six resealable sandwich bags
- small plastic container (with lid)
- plastic eye dropper
- small plastic cup
- crayons
- watercolor paints and paintbrush
- paper towels

Shoe Box Setup

Copy a supply of the record sheet. Write "Yes" on one lid and "No" on the other. Place each set of squares in a plastic bag and label the bag accordingly (Sponge, Paper, Plastic, Cloth, Foil, Waxed Paper). Label the plastic container "Used." Place the record sheets, lids, bags, eye dropper, plastic cup, crayons, paints, paintbrush, container, and paper towels in the shoe box. Glue the label to one end of the box and the student directions to the inside of the lid.

TIPS

- Tell students that when a material *absorbs* liquid, it "drinks" the liquid, or soaks it up. Explain that *nonabsorbent* materials *repel* liquid—they force it away. Instead of soaking into the material, the liquid beads up or rolls off.

- Based on their experiences, have students identify items in the classroom as absorbent (sponge, paper, soil for a plant) or nonabsorbent (rain jacket, vinyl mat, spoons).

Physical Science: Absorbency

Is It Thirsty?

Directions

1. Place the Yes and No lids faceup. Fill the cup halfway with water.

2. Take a square from one bag. Predict: Will it absorb water? Place the square on Yes or No to show your answer.

3. Test the square. Use the dropper to put a drop of water on the square.

4. Does it absorb water? Circle your answer on a record sheet. Then put the square in the Used container.

5. Repeat steps 2 through 4 to test each material.

6. Complete the activity at the bottom of your record sheet.

Is It Thirsty? Record Sheet

Name_____ Date_____

Does it **absorb** water? Circle **yes** or **no**.

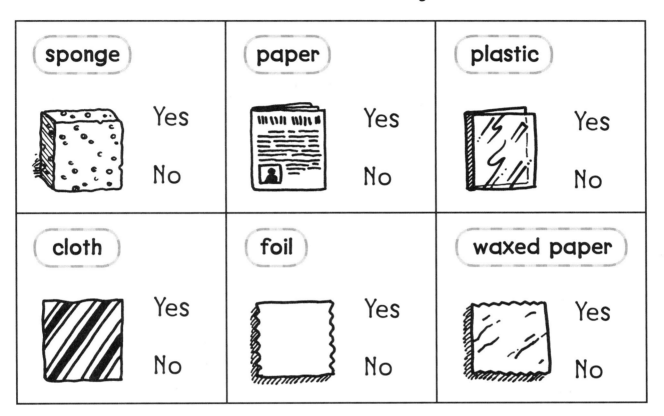

sponge	paper	plastic
Yes / No	Yes / No	Yes / No
cloth	foil	waxed paper
Yes / No	Yes / No	Yes / No

Try This

① Color one side of the shape with a crayon.

② Paint the whole shape. Watch what happens.

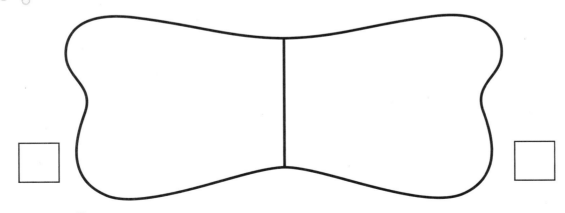

③ Which side **repels** the wet paint? Put an **X** in that box.

Shadow Show

Children explore shadows and light with transparent, translucent, and opaque objects.

Materials

- shoe box
- box label
- student directions
- record sheet (page 51)
- white construction paper
- glue stick
- six objects:

    transparent: clear plastic sandwich bag; small, clear plastic jar

    translucent: plastic bowl; unscented dryer sheet

    opaque: wood block; jar lid

- flashlight

Shoe Box Setup

Copy a supply of the record sheet. Trim the sheet of white construction paper to fit inside the bottom of the shoe box. Glue it in place. Place the objects, flashlight, and record sheets in the shoe box. Glue the label to one end of the box and the student directions to the inside of the lid.

○ ° ○ TIPS ○ ° ○

- Share *What Makes a Shadow?* by Clyde Robert Bulla (Scholastic, 1998), or a similar book.

- Discuss how shadows are made and teach related vocabulary (*transparent*, *translucent*, and *opaque*). Explain that it takes a light source and an object to make (or cast) a shadow. Point out that not all objects cast dark shadows.

Physical Science: Light and Shadows

Shadow Show

Directions
(For partners)

1. Empty the shoe box and stand it up with the opening facing you. Complete the activity with your partner. Each partner fills out a record sheet.

2. Choose an object. Predict: What kind of shadow will it make? Mark your prediction on your record sheet with an X.

3. One partner holds the object in front of the box. The other partner shines the flashlight on it.

4. What kind of shadow does it make? Circle the result.

5. Repeat steps 2 through 4 for each object. Take turns with your partner holding the object and shining the flashlight. Keep going until you complete your record sheets.

Shadow Show: Record Sheet

Name_____ Date_____

What kind of shadow will each object cast?

Object	1. **X** the box for your **prediction**. 2. Circle your **result**.
jar	☐ black ☐ gray ☐ white
lid	☐ black ☐ gray ☐ white
dryer sheet	☐ black ☐ gray ☐ white
sandwich bag	☐ black ☐ gray ☐ white
bowl	☐ black ☐ gray ☐ white
block	☐ black ☐ gray ☐ white

Spin a Color

Children spin color wheels to explore how different colors combine to make new colors.

Materials

- shoe box
- box label
- student directions
- color wheel patterns (page 53)
- record sheet and answer key (page 54)
- tagboard
- crayons (red, blue, yellow, green, orange, purple, black, brown)
- five wooden pencils with erasers (blunt the tips)
- 10 rubber bands

Shoe Box Setup

Make five copies of the color wheel patterns. Copy the answer key and a supply of record sheets. Color the wheels as follows, alternating the colors around each wheel: (1) red/blue; (2) red/yellow; (3) yellow/blue; (4) red/green/blue; (5) green/red/orange. Cut out the color wheels, glue to tagboard, and trim to size. Assemble the color wheels, as shown on page 53. To complete the answer key, fill in the colors as indicated for each color wheel. Place the color wheels, answer key, record sheets, and crayons in the shoe box. Glue the label to one end of the box and the student directions to the inside of the lid.

○ ° ○ TIPS ○ ° ○

- Share *Mouse Paint* by Ellen Stoll Walsh (Harcourt, 1989), or another "color-mixing" story.
- Explain that a ray of light has all of the rainbow colors. But we only see the colors of light that bounce off of an object. For example, only red light bounces off of a red fire truck.
- Model how to spin a wheel, like a top, and let children practice before completing the center activity.

Physical Science: Color Combinations

Spin a Color

Directions

1 Choose a two-color wheel. Color the first wheel under Wheel Colors on your record sheet to match.

2 Predict: What color will you see when you spin the wheel? Fill in the color under Prediction.

3 Spin the wheel. What color did you see? Fill in the color under Results.

4 Repeat steps 1, 2, and 3 for each two-color wheel.

5 Now follow the same steps to test the three-color wheels.

6 Complete the record sheet. Use the Answer Key to check your work.

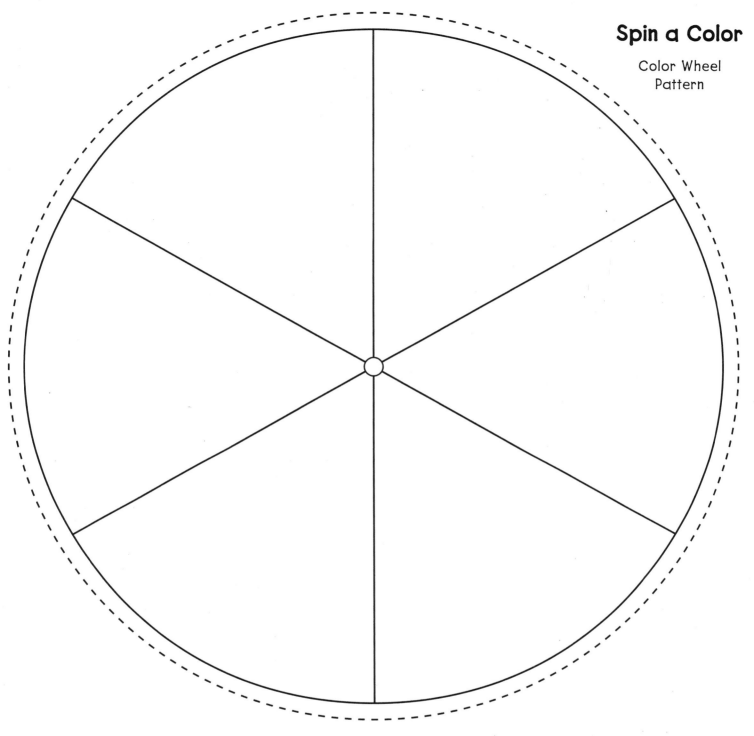

Spin a Color

Color Wheel
Pattern

Spinner Assembly

(1) Push the pencil tip through the center of the spinner (extending about an inch).

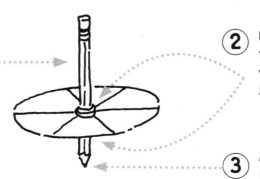

(2) Loop a rubber band around the pencil just above the wheel and another one just below the wheel.

(3) Make sure the pencil tip is blunt.

Spin a Color: Record Sheet

Name_____ Date_____

Wheel Colors	Prediction	Result
1 ⊛	◯	◯
2 ⊛	◯	◯
3 ⊛	◯	◯
4 ⊛	◯	◯
5 ⊛	◯	◯

Spin a Color: Answer Key

Wheel Colors	Result
⊛	◯
⊛	◯
⊛	◯
⊛	◯
⊛	◯

Good Vibrations

Children play instruments to explore how vibrations work to make sounds.

Materials

- shoe box
- box label
- student directions
- record sheet (page 56)
- small, cardboard jewelry box, without lid
- two rubber bands
- yogurt cup
- coffee filter
- craft stick
- crayons

Shoe Box Setup

Copy a supply of record sheets. To make each instrument:

- **Guitar:** Stretch a rubber band around the box.
- **Drum:** Place the coffee filter over the yogurt cup. Secure with a rubber band. Make sure the filter is tight and smooth.

Place the record sheets, instruments, craft stick, and crayons in the shoe box. Glue the label to one end of the box and the student directions to the inside of the lid.

° ° ° TIPS ° ° °

- Explain that when an instrument is played, it makes vibrations (sound waves) that travel through the air. These sound waves enter the ear, where nerves let the brain know that a sound was made.
- Extend the activity by having students make their own instruments. Provide suitable materials, such as cardboard tubes and boxes, canisters, pie pans, coffee filters, rubber bands, and craft sticks.

Physical Science: Sound

Good Vibrations

Directions
(For partners)

1. Take turns following steps 2, 3, and 4 for each instrument.

2. Choose an instrument. Predict: Will you 👁 see, 👂 hear, and ✋ feel the vibrations? Underline the pictures on the record sheet to show your prediction.

3. Play the instrument by following the directions below.

4. Were you able to 👁 see, 👂 hear, and ✋ feel the vibrations? Circle the pictures on the record sheet to show your results.

Guitar: Snap the rubber band.

Drum: Tap the drum with the stick.

Good Vibrations: Record Sheet

Name _____

Date _____

Instrument	I predict I will...	I was able to...
guitar	👁 see 👂 hear ✋ feel the vibrations.	👁 see 👂 hear ✋ feel the vibrations.
drum	👁 see 👂 hear ✋ feel the vibrations.	👁 see 👂 hear ✋ feel the vibrations.

Shoe Box Learning Centers: Science © 2012 by Immacula A. Rhodes, Scholastic Teaching Resources

Going Up!

Children explore how three simple machines are used to move objects.

Materials

- shoe box
- box label
- student directions
- record sheet (page 58)
- 12-inch wood ruler
- 2 beanbags
- sturdy cardboard
  (about 4 by 11 inches)
- wide, clear packing tape
- metal binder clip
- 3-foot length of string
- student scissors
- glue stick

Shoe Box Setup

Copy a supply of record sheets. For use with the inclined plane, tie the string to the binder clip, then attach the clip to a beanbag (as shown, right). Place the record sheets, beanbags (load), ruler (for lever setup), cardboard (for inclined plane setup), scissors, and glue stick in the shoe box. Glue the label to one end of the box and the student directions to the inside of the lid.

TIPS

- Discuss and demonstrate how each simple machine can be used to move objects up and down. Brainstorm real-life examples of each machine, including those on page 58:

    slide and ramp (inclined plane)
    seesaw and hammer (lever)

- Teach vocabulary related to the center activity, including *inclined plane*, *lever*, and *load*. You may also wish to introduce more challenging vocabulary, such as *fulcrum*.

Physical Science: Simple Machines

Going Up!

Directions (For partners)

1. Take turns with your partner completing steps 2 and 3. Each partner fills out a record sheet as you go.

2. Lift the beanbag by hand. Then test the inclined plane.

    Inclined Plane: Empty the shoe box and turn it upside down. Set up the cardboard to match the picture. Have your partner hold the shoe box steady. Use the string to pull the beanbag up the cardboard.

3. Lift the beanbag by hand again. Then test the lever.

    Lever: Set up the ruler and beanbag to match the picture. Push down on the ruler to lift the beanbag.

4. Look at each picture.

    Cut out the pictures on your record sheet. Glue each picture where it belongs.

Going Up! Record Sheet

Name _____

Date _____

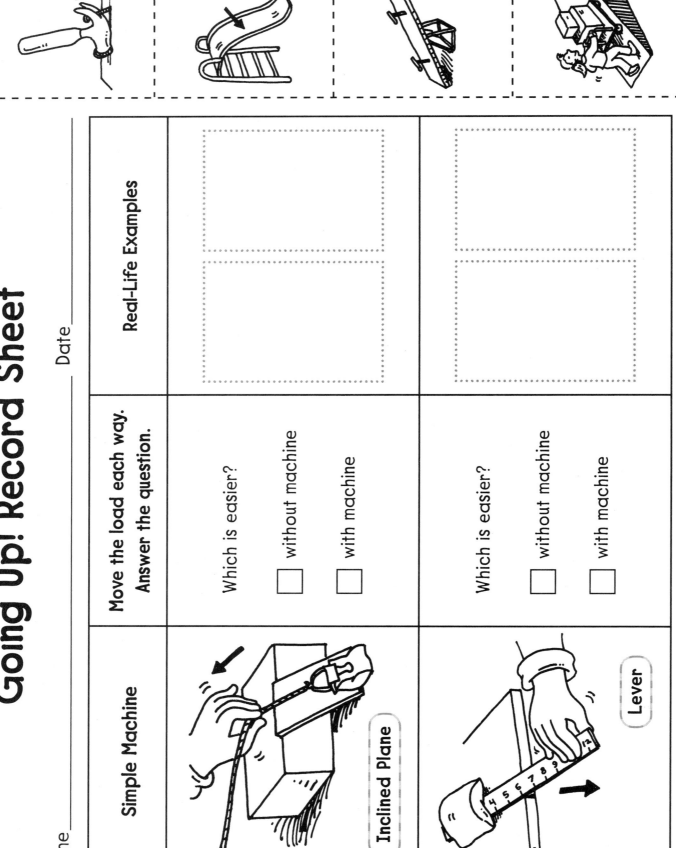

Simple Machine	Move the load each way. Answer the question.	Real-Life Examples
Inclined Plane	Which is easier? ☐ without machine ☐ with machine	
Lever	Which is easier? ☐ without machine ☐ with machine	

What's the Matter?

Children classify pictures to demonstrate understanding of the three states of matter.

Materials

- shoe box
- box label
- student directions
- activity mat (page 60)
- picture cards and mat labels (page 61)
- answer key (See Shoe Box Setup)
- page-protector sleeves

Shoe Box Setup

Copy the activity mat three times. Then copy, color, and cut apart the picture cards and mat labels. Glue a label ("Solids," "Liquids," "Gases") to each mat. To make the answer key, prepare a duplicate set of the copied components. Glue each picture card to the corresponding mat. Then slip each completed mat into a page-protector sleeve. Put the activity mats, picture cards, and answer key in the shoe box. Glue the label to one end of the box and the student directions to the inside of the lid.

TIPS

- Share *What Is the World Made Of? All About Solids, Liquids, and Gases* by Kathleen Weidner Zoehfeld (HarperCollins, 1998), or a similar book.

- Explain that everything in our world is made of matter. The three states of matter are *solid*, *liquid*, and *gas*. Review the properties of each:

  A **solid** has a specific shape. Its shape does not change unless something happens to it (such as reshaping a playdough figure).

  A **liquid** takes the shape of its container (like water in a pitcher). It will flow if it is not contained or if it is poured.

  A **gas** flows and fills up its container (such as helium in a balloon). If not contained, a gas will spread through the air. Most gases are invisible.

Physical Science: States of Matter

What's the Matter?

Directions
(For partners)

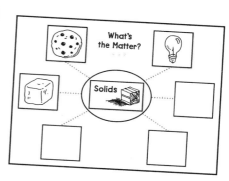

1. Place the mats faceup. Spread out the cards facedown.

2. One partner chooses a card and follows these steps:
   - Name the picture.
   - What state of matter does it show? Tell your partner and explain how you know.
   - Place the card on the matching mat.

3. Partners take turns repeating step 2, until all of the cards have been used.

4. Use the Answer Key to check your work.

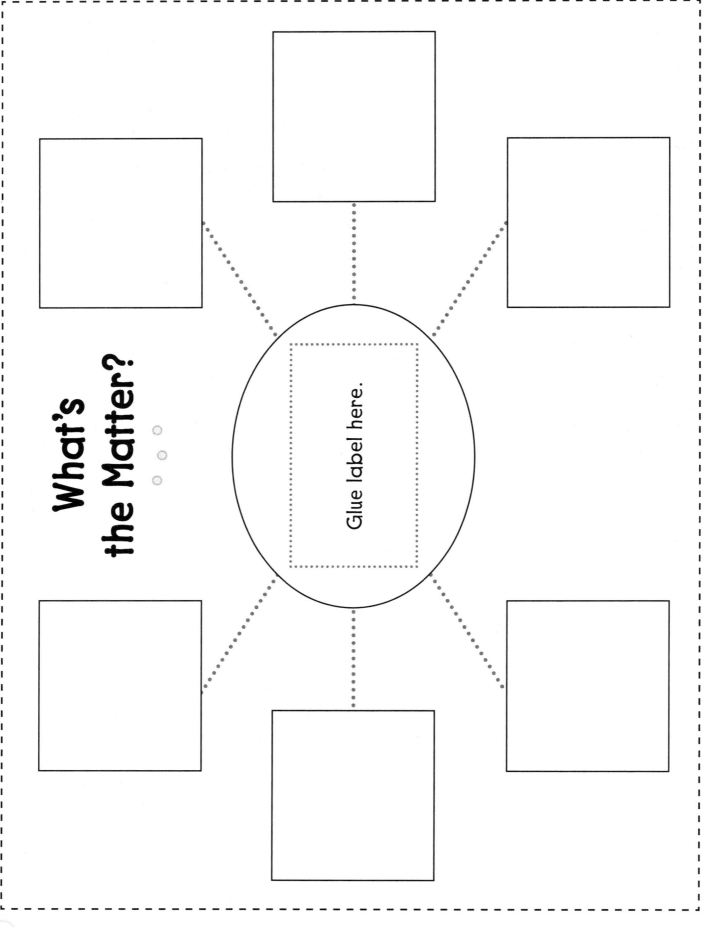

What's the Matter?

Glue label here.

What's the Matter?

Picture Cards and Mat Labels

Solids

Liquids

Gases

Signs of the Seasons

Children identify and sort scenes and events related to each season of the year.

Materials

- shoe box
- box label
- student directions
- picture cards and season labels (page 63)
- construction paper (white, light green, light blue, orange)
- season mats (see Shoe Box Setup)
- answer key (see Shoe Box Setup)
- page-protector sleeves
- crayons

Shoe Box Setup

Copy, color, and cut apart the picture cards and season labels. Cut the construction paper into 7-inch circles (one of each color per student). Cut an extra two of each color to make the season mats and answer key. **Season mats:** Glue the labels to a set of construction-paper circles as follows: Winter, white; Spring, green; Summer, blue; Fall, orange. **Answer key:** Copy another set of picture cards and prepare an extra set of season mats as above. Glue the picture cards to the corresponding season mats and slip them into page-protector sleeves. Place the season mats, picture cards, supply of colored circles, answer key, and crayons in the shoe box. Glue the label to one end of the box and the student directions to the inside of the lid.

° ° ° TIPS ° ° °

- Review that seasons follow the same cycle every year. Discuss signs of nature related to each season, such as falling snow and hibernating animals (winter), sprouting plants and hatching chicks (spring), maturing animals and blooming trees (summer), and falling leaves and migrating animals (fall).

- Review the picture cards and the seasons they represent. Discuss *hibernation* and *migration*, using the corresponding cards. Point out that not all seasonal changes occur in every area of the country. For example, snow rarely falls in regions far south.

Earth Science: Seasons

Signs of the Seasons

Directions

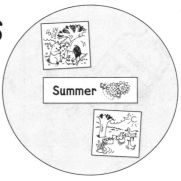

① Place the season mats and picture cards faceup.

② Sort all the bear pictures into one group. Then sort the remaining cards into groups. There are four cards for each group.

③ Take one group of cards. Match each card to the mat for its season. Use the Answer Key to check your work.

④ Repeat step 3 to sort each group of cards.

⑤ Make your own season mats. Take a circle of each color. Write the season on each circle. Draw things that go with that season.

Winter

Summer

Spring

Fall

Wonderful Wind

Children blow a variety of objects to explore the power of wind to move things.

Materials

- shoe box
- box label
- student directions
- record sheet (page 65)
- small, paperback book
- copy paper, folded in half twice
- two small plastic cups
- two spoonfuls of sand (seal in snack-size resealable bag; press air out)
- wide, clear tape
- thin, cotton fabric (cut into two 7-inch squares)
- cotton ball
- eight pennies
- yarn
- crayons

Shoe Box Setup

Copy a supply of record sheets. Use a rolled piece of tape to attach the bag of sand to the inside bottom of one cup. Place the cotton ball in the center of a fabric square, pull up the corners toward the middle, and tie with a piece of yarn to create a small pouch. Flatten the bottom so the pouch stands upright. Repeat, using the pennies and other fabric square. Place the record sheets, book, folded paper, cups, pouches, and crayons in the shoe box. Glue the label to one end of the box and the student directions to the inside of the lid.

∘ ∘ ∘ TIPS ∘ ∘ ∘

- Share *Feel the Wind* by Arthur Dorros (HarperCollins, 1990), or a similar book.
- Explain that when the sun warms the air, that air rises and cool air takes its place. This movement of air is what makes the wind. Tell students that slow-moving air creates a gentle wind. Fast-moving air makes a strong wind.

Earth Science: Weather

Wonderful Wind

Directions

1. Pick up each cup. Compare the weight of each.

2. Place the cups near the edge of a table.

3. Blow air at each cup. Blow gently. Did the lighter cup move? Did the heavier cup move?

4. Blow again. This time, blow hard! What happened?

5. Repeat steps 1 through 4 using the two pouches. Then use the book and folded paper.

6. Complete a record sheet.

Wonderful Wind: Record Sheet

Name _____

Date _____

Draw something each kind of wind can move.

Gentle Wind

Strong Wind

Gentle Winds	Strong Winds	
☐	☐	are quiet.
☐	☐	are not quiet.
☐	☐	move heavy things.
☐	☐	move lightweight things.
☐	☐	move slowly.
☐	☐	move fast.

Shoe Box Learning Centers: Science © 2012 by Immacula A. Rhodes, Scholastic Teaching Resources

Water Everywhere!

As children play a game, they identify examples of precipitation, evaporation, and condensation.

Materials

- shoe box
- box label
- student directions
- game boards (pages 67–68)
- spinner pattern (page 69)
- brass fastener
- bingo markers (15 in each of two colors)
- three half-sheets of construction paper (any color)
- answer key (see Shoe Box Setup)
- page-protector sleeves

Shoe Box Setup

Copy and color the game boards and spinner pattern. Cut out the spinner patterns and assemble as shown on page 69. If possible, laminate game boards and spinner for durability. To make the answer key, label each half-sheet of paper with a water-cycle stage (*evaporation, precipitation, condensation*). Cut out the pictures on an extra copy of each game board and glue to the corresponding water-cycle sheet. (See list, page 69.) Slip the answer-key pages into page-protector sleeves. Place the game boards, spinner, bingo markers (game markers), and answer key in the shoe box. Glue the label to one end of the box and the student directions to the inside of the lid.

○ ○ ○ **TIPS** ○ ○ ○

- Share *Down Comes the Rain* by Franklyn M. Branley (HarperCollins, 1997), or a similar book. Discuss the stages of the water cycle:

  Precipitation is water that falls from clouds in the form of rain, snow, sleet, or hail.

  Evaporation occurs when the sun heats water and turns it into vapor or steam.

  Condensation occurs when cold air turns water vapor back into a liquid that collects in clouds. When the air can't hold the condensed water any longer, it falls to the earth as precipitation.

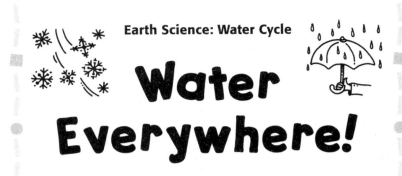

Earth Science: Water Cycle

Water Everywhere!

Directions
(For 2 players)

1. Each player takes a game board and set of markers. Players take turns following steps 2, 3, and 4.

2. Spin the spinner. What letter did it land on? Find the letter on your game board.

3. What stage of the water cycle did the spinner land on? Find a picture for that stage in the column under your letter.

4. Check the Answer Key. If correct, place a marker on the picture.

5. Keep taking turns. The first one to cover all five boxes in any row wins the game.

Water Everywhere! • Game Board 1

	W	A	T	E	R

Shoe Box Learning Centers: Science © 2012 by Immacula A. Rhodes, Scholastic Teaching Resources

Water Everywhere!

W	A	T	E	R

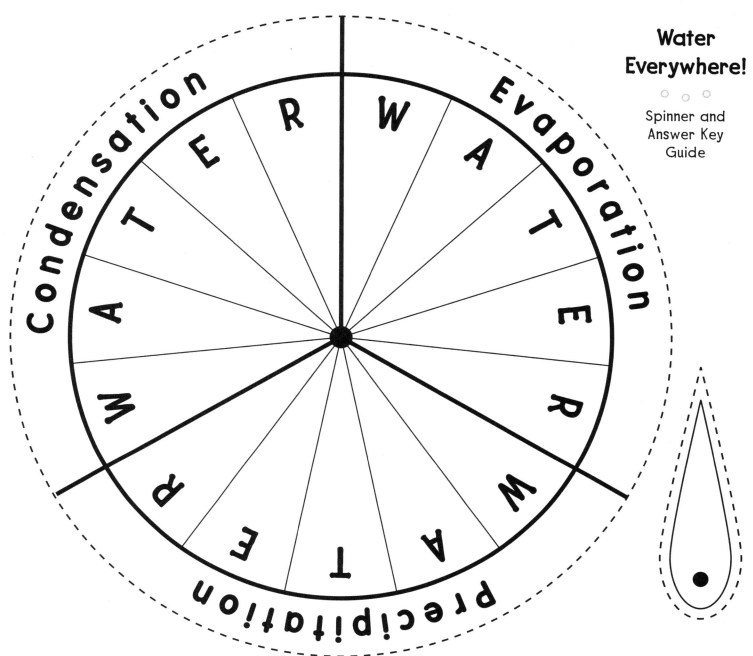

Use the following as a guide for making the Answer Key:

Precipitation

- hail
- rain mist
- rain shower
- sleet
- snow

Condensation

- cloud
- dew on grass
- foggy mountains
- foggy window

Evaporation

- steamy lake
- steamy road
- shrinking puddle

Assemble the spinner using a brass fastener as shown. Laminate the water drop so it spins easily. If you do not laminate, glue a paper clip to the back of the water drop, then insert brass fastener. Make sure the spinner moves easily.

Measuring Weather

Children explore how weather tools are used to measure various weather conditions.

Materials

- shoe box
- box label
- student directions
- wind vane patterns and record sheet (page 71)
- small container half-filled with playdough (with lid)
- wooden pencil with eraser (blunt the tip)
- marker cap (from dried-out marker)
- craft glue
- clear, 10-ounce plastic cup
- ruler
- thermometer (non-mercury)
- crayons

Shoe Box Setup

Copy a supply of record sheets. Copy the wind vane patterns and glue to tagboard, then cut out each part. Cut a small hole in the center of the playdough-container lid. Complete the wind vane assembly as shown on page 71. To make the rain gauge, mark inch and half-inch increments—up to 3 inches—on the outside of the plastic cup. Label only the inch marks. Place the record sheets, wind vane, rain gauge, thermometer, and crayons in the shoe box. Glue the label to one end of the box and the student directions to the inside of the lid.

◦ ◦ ◦ TIPS ◦ ◦ ◦

- Explain that scientists use many tools, such as the following, to measure weather:

  Rain gauge: Collects rain and is used to measure how much rain has fallen.

  Wind vane: Measures wind direction. In nature, the wind makes the vane spin. In which direction did the "wind" blow?

  Thermometer: Measures temperature and is used to tell how hot or cold the air or water is.

Earth Science: Weather Tools

Measuring Weather

Directions
(For partners)

1. Take turns with your partner in each step. Fill out a record sheet as you go.

2. **Wind vane:** Blow on the arrow. Let it stop spinning. In which direction is the "wind" blowing?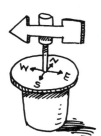

3. **Rain gauge:** Choose a measurement. Put that amount of "rain" in the gauge. Empty it and repeat.

4. **Thermometer:** Take the air temperature. Then put water in the rain gauge. Take the water temperature.

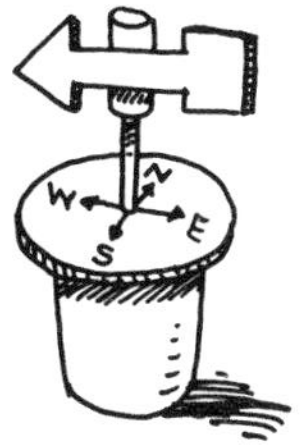

Measuring Weather

Name _____ Date _____

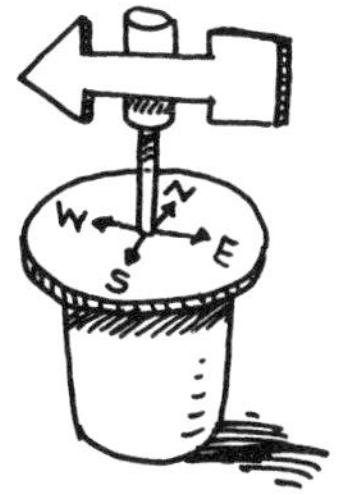

Draw an arrow on the compass rose to show your answer.

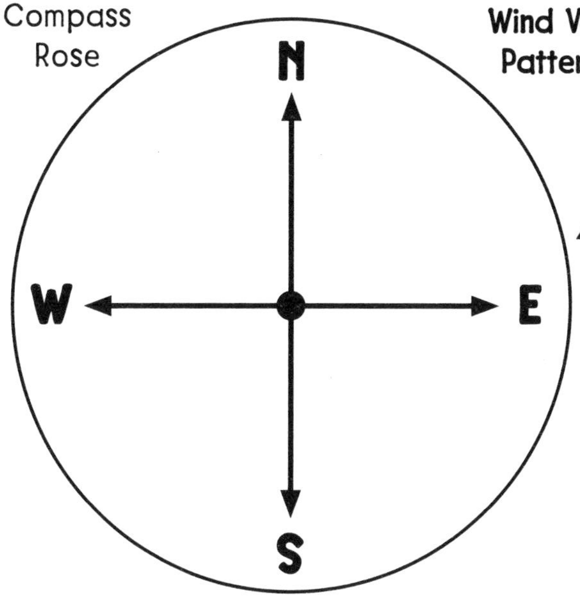

① N E W S

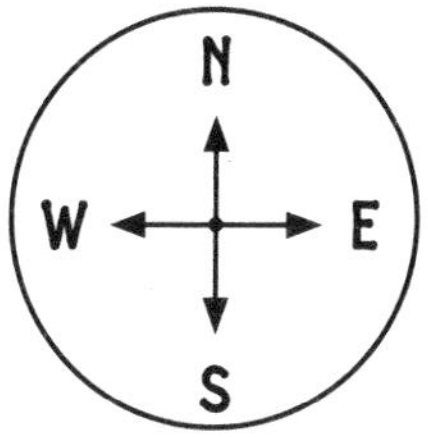

② N E W S

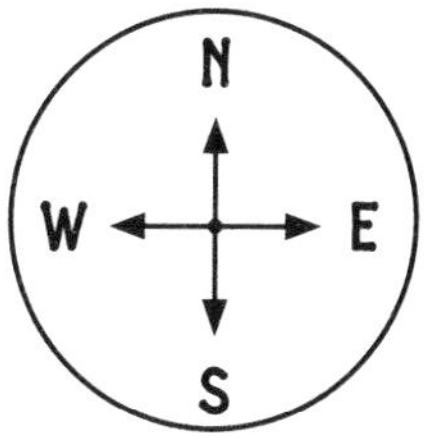

Draw the water line.

① $2\frac{1}{2}$ inches

② $\frac{1}{2}$ inch

① 1 inch

② 2 inches

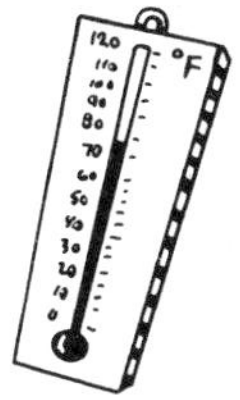

Write each temperature.

① Air temperature: _____ °F

② Water temperature: _____ °F

Shoe Box Learning Centers: Science © 2012 by Immacula A. Rhodes, Scholastic Teaching Resources

---

Wind Vane Patterns

Compass Rose

N E S W

Arrow

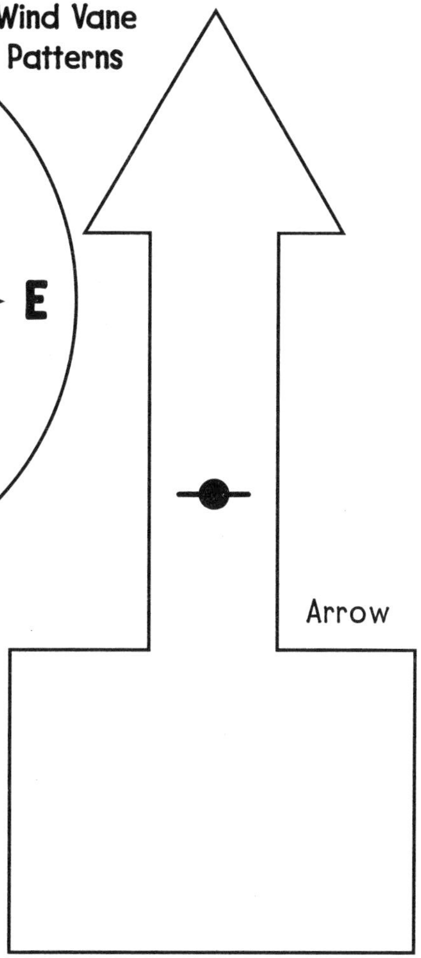

How to Assemble:

① Glue marker cap to arrow at dot.

② Poke the pencil through the compass rose, then the container lid.

③ Push pencil to bottom of container. Snap on the lid.

④ Place the marker cap over the pencil eraser to attach the arrow.

In the Sky

Children play a game to test their knowledge about Sun, Earth, and Moon facts.

Materials

- shoe box
- box label
- student directions
- fact cards (page 73)
- activity mat and connect-the-dot puzzle (page 74)
- answer key (see Shoe Box Setup)
- page-protector sleeves
- crayons

Shoe Box Setup

Copy and cut apart the fact cards and activity mat. Copy a supply of the connect-the-dot puzzle. To create an answer key, make an extra copy of the fact cards and mat. Cut out the Sun, Earth, and Moon sections from the activity mat and glue each to the top of a separate sheet of paper. Fill in the answer on each card, then glue the cards to the corresponding pages. Slip the answer-key pages into page-protector sleeves. Place the activity mat, fact cards, connect-the-dot puzzles, crayons, and answer key in the shoe box. Glue the label to one end of the box and the students directions to the inside of the lid.

◦ ◦ ◦ TIPS ◦ ◦ ◦

- Share *What Makes Day and Night* by Franklyn M. Branley (HarperCollins, 1986), or a similar book. Discuss the importance of the Sun, Earth, and Moon, and how they work together.

- Review the fact cards. Challenge students to fill in the blanks as you read each one. Then create a Venn diagram to compare the characteristics of the Sun, Earth, and Moon. Encourage students to share additional facts about each of the space bodies.

- When introducing this center, review the Connect-the-Dots Puzzle. Explain to children that as they play, they will connect the dots to make a picture of something else they can see in the sky. When children have completed the puzzle, review with them that it is a picture of the Big Dipper.

Earth Science: Space

In the Sky

Directions

(For 2 players)

1. Shuffle the cards. Stack them facedown near the mat. Take turns following steps 3, 4, and 5.

2. Each player takes his or her own connect-the-dot puzzle.

3. Take the top card. Read the fact.

4. Is the fact about the Sun, the Earth, or the Moon? Tell your answer.

5. Check the Answer Key.
   - If correct, put the card on the mat. Then connect two stars on your puzzle.
   - If not, put the card on the bottom of the stack.

6. Keep taking turns. The first one to complete a puzzle wins the game.

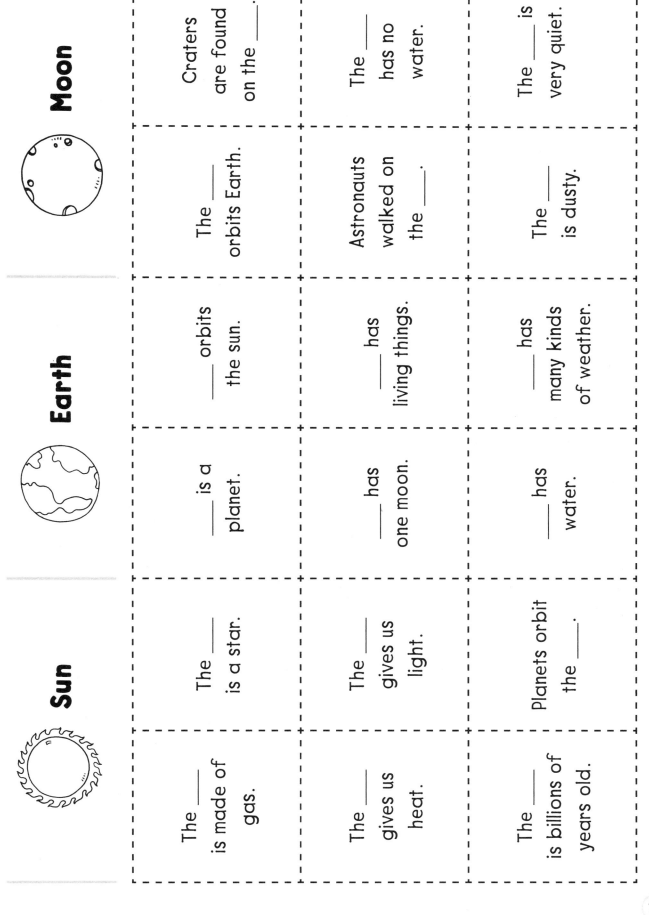

Sun

Earth

Moon

The ___ is made of gas.

The ___ gives us heat.

The ___ is billions of years old.

The ___ is a star.

The ___ gives us light.

Planets orbit the ___.

___ is a planet.

___ has one moon.

___ has water.

___ orbits the sun.

___ has living things.

___ has many kinds of weather.

The ___ orbits Earth.

Astronauts walked on the ___.

The ___ is dusty.

Craters are found on the ___.

The ___ has no water.

The ___ is very quiet.

Shoe Box Learning Centers: Science © 2012 by Immacula A. Rhodes, Scholastic Teaching Resources

In the Sky Activity Mat

Sun

Earth

Moon

Stack used Sun cards here.	Stack used Earth cards here.	Stack used Moon cards here.

In the Sky ● Connect-the-Dots Puzzle

Name_____ Date_____

Connect the stars as you play. What did you make?

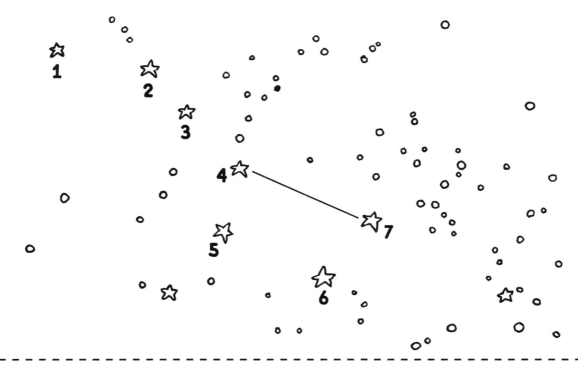

Moon Prints

Children create craters in "moon sand" to explore how they are made on the Moon.

Materials

- plastic shoe box with removable lid
- box label
- student directions
- record sheet (page 76)
- gallon-size resealable plastic bag (for record sheets)
- large, plastic mixing bowl
- four cups of sand
- two cups of cornstarch
- $\frac{1}{4}$ cup of water
- rubber superball, ping-pong ball, golf ball, tennis ball
- 6-inch length of yarn
- fork (to loosen and level moon sand)

Shoe Box Setup

Copy a supply of record sheets. Place them in the plastic bag and seal. To make "moon sand," mix the sand and cornstarch together in the bowl. Add water gradually—a little at a time—mixing thoroughly to create a soft and moist (but loose) mixture. Place the moon sand in the plastic shoe box. Add the record sheets, balls, yarn, and fork. Tape the label to one end of the box and the student directions to the inside of the lid.

TIPS

- Share *The Magic School Bus Takes a Moonwalk* by Joanna Cole (Scholastic Inc., 2004), or a similar book.
- Explain that craters form when a meteorite hits the moon's surface. The size and depth of a crater depends on the meteorite's mass, speed, and angle of impact.
- When modeling the center, demonstrate how to loosen the moon sand and rake the surface with the fork to smooth it out.

Earth Science: Space

Moon Prints

Directions

1. Place the shoe box on the floor. Set the cover aside. Take out the balls, yarn, record sheets, and fork.

2. Kneel beside the box. Take the first two balls pictured on your record sheet.

3. Hold the balls at the same height over the sand. Now drop them.

4. Take each ball out of the sand.
   - Use the yarn to measure across the craters.
   - Look to see which crater is deeper.
   - Check ✔ the boxes on your record sheet to show your results.

5. Smooth out the sand. Repeat steps 2, 3, and 4 with the next two balls. Complete your record sheet.

Moon Prints: Record Sheet

Name_____ Date_____

Balls	Craters	
Make craters. Drop each ball.	Measure across. Which is wider?	Look. Which is deeper?
(1) tennis ball		
golf ball		
(2) ping-pong ball		
superball		

Astronauts left footprints on the moon!
What prints would you leave on the moon? Draw them!

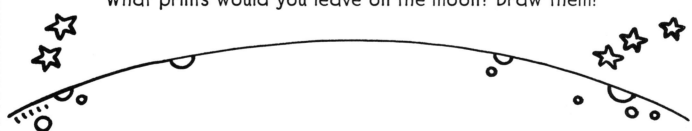

Ready to Rock!

Children examine and sort rocks to discover their various attributes.

Materials

- shoe box
- box label
- student directions
- 9- by 12-inch sheet of construction paper (any color)
- yarn
- craft glue
- unlined 4- by 6-inch index cards, cut into fourths
- marker
- small rocks in various colors and textures

Shoe Box Setup

To make an activity mat, laminate the construction paper. Then glue yarn on the laminated paper to create two 6-inch overlapping circles (Venn diagram). Examine the rocks to determine some common attributes among them, such as colors (black, white, pink), patterns (stripes, spots, swirls), and textures (rough, smooth, bumpy). Write the attributes on the index cards (one per card). Write "Both" on another index card to create a label for the overlapping area of the mat. Place the activity mat, word cards, and rocks in the shoe box. Glue the label to one end of the box and the student directions to the inside of the lid.

° ° ° TIPS ° ° °

- Share *Let's Go Rock Collecting* by Roma Gans (HarperCollins, 1997), or a similar book. Display several rocks and discuss the many different colors and textures rocks can have.

- Explain the three ways rocks are formed: **Igneous** rocks start as melted rock that gets pushed up to the earth's surface and then cools and hardens. **Sedimentary** rocks form from layers of sand, mud, and pebbles that get pressed together and harden. **Metamorphic** rocks change from one kind of rock to another due to heat and pressure.

Earth Science: Rocks

Ready to Rock!

Directions
(For partners)

① Place the activity mat faceup. Put the "Both" card where the circles overlap.

② Take two cards. Place one next to each circle.

③ Choose a rock with your partner and look at it.

- Does it match one of the words? If so, place it in that circle.
- Does it match both of the words? If so, place it under "Both."

④ Repeat step 3 with all of the rocks.

⑤ Clear the mat. Then repeat steps 2, 3, and 4 to work with new cards.

Earth's Gifts

Children discover that people use natural resources for many different things.

Materials

- shoe box
- box label
- student directions
- picture cards and sentence strips (page 79)
- mini-book pages (page 80)
- resealable bag
- paper clips
- student scissors
- glue stick
- crayons
- stapler

Shoe Box Setup

Copy the picture cards (class set plus one extra) and sentence strips (one set). For self-checking, label the backs of the extra picture cards with the natural resource (trees, rocks, water, wind), then laminate. Cut apart these cards and place them in a resealable bag. Copy and cut apart the mini-book cover and page. Copy a class set of the cover. Make four copies of the mini-book page and glue a sentence strip to each in the space indicated at the top. Copy a class supply of those pages, then clip together sets of the mini-book pages (cover plus four interior pages). Place the picture cards, mini-book sets, student scissors, glue, crayons, and stapler in the shoe box. Glue the label to one end of the box and the student directions to the inside of the lid.

TIPS

- Explain that a natural resource is something made from nature that people and animals use. Water, trees and plants, rocks and soil, wind, and fossil fuels are all examples of natural resources. Work with children to make a list of things that come from Earth's resources.

- Discuss the importance of natural resources to life on Earth and the need to protect and manage them wisely. Talk about ways students use and can help conserve natural resources at home and school.

Earth Science: Natural Resources

Earth's Gifts

Directions

(1) Take the picture cards out of the bag. Spread out a set of mini-book pages. Write your name on the cover.

(2) Choose a card and name it. What natural resource does it come from? Place the card on that mini-book page.

(3) Repeat Step 2 with all of the cards. Then check your answers on the back. Move cards if you need to.

(4) Take a page of picture cards and cut them out. Match your pictures to the cards on the pages. Glue your pictures in place. Put away the first set of cards as you go.

(5) Draw one more picture on each page.

(6) Staple your pages to the cover. Read your book!

rocks	trees	water	wind

Earth gives us rocks for many things.

Earth gives us trees for many things.

Earth gives us water for many things.

Earth gives us wind for many things.

Shoe Box Learning Centers: Science © 2012 by Immacula A. Rhodes, Scholastic Teaching Resources

Earth's Gifts

by _____

Draw one more thing.